Mastering HTML: Learning Beyond the Basics

Table of Contents

Learning Objectives

By the end of this book, you will be able to:

1. **Understand the Fundamentals of HTML5**
   - Explain the purpose and benefits of HTML5 in modern web development.
   - Identify key differences between HTML5 and previous versions of HTML.
2. **Utilize HTML5 Tags and Structure Effectively**
   - Recognize commonly used HTML5 tags and their functions.
   - Implement best practices for writing clean and well-structured HTML code.
3. **Leverage New HTML5 Elements for Improved Semantics**
   - Use elements like <article>, <section>, <header>, and <footer> to organize web content.
   - Enhance webpage accessibility and SEO using semantic tags.
4. **Implement HTML5 Event Attributes for Interactivity**

     ○ Apply event attributes such as onclick, onmouseover, and onchange to enhance user engagement.
     ○ Create dynamic and responsive web pages using event-driven actions.

5. **Integrate Google Maps into Web Pages**
   ○ Embed Google Maps using HTML5 and JavaScript APIs.
   ○ Customize map features and add location-based functionalities.

6. **Apply Semantic HTML5 Elements for Better Accessibility**
   ○ Understand the role of semantic tags in improving readability and usability.
   ○ Ensure websites comply with accessibility standards for inclusive user experiences.

7. **Migrate from Older HTML Versions to HTML5**
   ○ Upgrade existing web pages to HTML5 while maintaining compatibility with older browsers.
   ○ Optimize HTML code for better performance and maintainability.

8. **Work with HTML5 Audio Elements**
   ○ Embed audio files using the <audio> element.
   ○ Customize playback controls and manage different audio formats.

9. **Implement Video Playback in HTML5**
   ○ Embed videos using the <video> element without relying on external plugins.
   ○ Ensure compatibility with different video formats and add captions for accessibility.

10. **Create and Manage Scalable Vector Graphics (SVG)**
    ○ Use the <svg> element to create sharp and scalable graphics.
    ○ Optimize SVG graphics for web applications.

11. **Utilize the HTML5 Canvas for Dynamic Graphics and Animations**
    ○ Draw and manipulate graphics using the <canvas> element and JavaScript.
    ○ Develop interactive visuals and animations for web applications.

12. **Apply Best Practices for HTML5 Development**
    ○ Write clean, efficient, and maintainable HTML5 code.
    ○ Follow industry standards for accessibility, responsiveness, and performance.

By mastering these learning objectives, you will gain the skills to build modern, interactive, and accessible web applications using HTML5.

Would you like any refinements or additions to better fit your learning goals?

A. Introduction to HTML5

What is HTML5?

HTML5 is the **latest version** of **HTML (HyperText Markup Language)**, which is used to create and structure web pages. It introduced new features that make websites more **interactive, responsive, and user-friendly** without relying on external plugins like Flash.

Example:

In HTML4, embedding a video required third-party plugins like Flash. In HTML5, you can use the <video> element to play videos directly in the browser:

```
<video controls>
    <source src="video.mp4" type="video/mp4">
    Your browser does not support the video tag.
</video>
```

Advantages of HTML5 over Older Versions:

- **No Need for Flash** – Videos and animations can be played directly in the browser.
- **Better Performance** – Faster loading times and improved user experience.
- **Mobile-Friendly** – Designed to work smoothly on phones, tablets, and desktops.

Key Features and Advancements of HTML5

HTML5 introduced several new features that make web development easier and more powerful.

Key Features with Examples:

1. **New Semantic Elements** – Improve webpage structure and SEO.
Example:

```
<header>Website Header</header>
<nav>Navigation Links</nav>
<section>Main Content</section>
<footer>Footer Information</footer>
```

Advantage: Helps search engines and screen readers understand webpage content better.

2. **Built-in Audio and Video Support** – No need for third-party plugins.
Example:
`<audio controls> <source src="audio.mp3" type="audio/mp3"> </audio>`
Advantage: Makes media playback faster and more efficient.

3. **Canvas and SVG for Graphics** – Create graphics directly in HTML.
Example:
`<canvas id="myCanvas" width="200" height="100" style="border:1px solid;"></canvas>`
Advantage: Allows drawing and animations without external software.

4. **Improved Forms with New Input Types** – Collect better user data.
Example:
`<input type="email" placeholder="Enter your email">`
`<input type="date">`
Advantage: Provides built-in validation and better user experience.

Why HTML5 Matters for Modern Web Development

HTML5 is essential for building modern websites and web applications. It improves user experience, supports multimedia, enhances performance, and ensures compatibility across devices.

Why HTML5 is Important:
- Better User Experience – Faster, interactive, and visually appealing websites.
- SEO & Accessibility – Helps search engines understand content better and makes sites accessible to all users.
- Cross-Device Compatibility – Works on desktops, tablets, and mobile phones.
- Improved Security – Reduces reliance on outdated technologies like Flash.

Example: Responsive Web Design

With HTML5 and CSS, websites automatically adjust to different screen sizes.
<meta name="viewport" content="width=device-width, initial-scale=1.0">

This ensures that the website looks good on both desktop and mobile devices.

Conclusion

HTML5 transformed web development by making sites faster, more interactive, and mobile-friendly. Whether creating a basic webpage or a complex app, HTML5 offers powerful tools for a modern and user-friendly experience.

B. HTML5 Tags and Structure

What Are HTML5 Tags?

HTML5 tags are elements used to structure and define different parts of a webpage. They help browsers and search engines understand content better while improving accessibility and readability.

Basic HTML5 Page Structure

A standard HTML5 webpage consists of the following key sections:

```
<!DOCTYPE html>
<html lang="en">
<head>
    <meta charset="UTF-8">
    <meta name="viewport" content="width=device-width, initial-scale=1.0">
    <title>My First HTML5 Page</title>
</head>
<body>
    <header>
        <h1>Welcome to My Website</h1>
    </header>
    <nav>
        <ul>
            <li><a href="#">Home</a></li>
            <li><a href="#">About</a></li>
            <li><a href="#">Contact</a></li>
        </ul>
    </nav>
```

```
<section>
    <h2>About HTML5</h2>
    <p>HTML5 is the latest version of HTML, introducing new elements and
features.</p>
    </section>
    <footer>
        <p>&copy; 2025 My Website. All rights reserved.</p>
    </footer>
</body>
</html>
```

Key HTML5 Structural Tags and Their Uses

Tag	Purpose	Example
`<header>`	Defines the top section, often containing a logo or title.	`<header><h1>Site Name</h1></header>`
`<nav>`	Contains navigation links.	`<nav><a href="#">Home</a></nav>`
`<section>`	Defines a thematic grouping of content.	`<section><h2>About Us</h2></section>`
`<article>`	Represents an independent, self-contained piece of content.	`<article><h2>Blog Post</h2></article>`
`<aside>`	Contains side content, like ads or related links.	`<aside><p>Related Articles</p></aside>`
`<footer>`	Defines the bottom section of a webpage.	`<footer><p>Copyright 2025</p></footer>`

How Tags Define Web Content

HTML5 tags describe the meaning and purpose of content to browsers, search engines, and assistive technologies (like screen readers).

Examples:

<h1> to <h6>: Define headings and improve readability.

<p>: Represents a paragraph.

<ul> and <ol>: Create unordered (bullet points) and ordered (numbered) lists.

<table>: Defines a table to display structured data.

Example: Defining Content with Tags

```
<section>
    <h2>Our Services</h2>
    <p>We offer web development, SEO, and graphic design services.</p>
    <ul>
        <li>Web Development</li>
        <li>SEO Optimization</li>
        <li>Graphic Design</li>
    </ul>
</section>
```

Why is this important?

- Improves webpage structure
- Helps search engines understand content
- Enhances accessibility for screen readers

Best Practices for Writing Clean HTML

To write efficient, readable, and well-structured HTML, follow these best practices:

Use Semantic HTML Tags

Instead of: <div class="header">Welcome</div>

Use: <header>Welcome</header>

✓ *Clearer meaning and better SEO*

Use Proper Nesting of Elements

Wrong way: <p><h2>Title</h2></p>

Correct way:

```
<h2>Title</h2>
<p>Paragraph text here.</p>
```

✓ *Avoids invalid HTML structure*

Indent Code for Readability

Messy Code:

<header><h1>Site Name</h1></header><section><h2>Content</h2></section>

Clean Code:

```
<header>
   <h1>Site Name</h1>
</header>
<section>
   <h2>Content</h2>
</section>
```

✓ *Easier to read and maintain*

Use Descriptive Attributes and Comments

Example:

```
<!-- Navigation Links -->
<nav>
   <a href="home.html">Home</a>
   <a href="about.html">About</a>
</nav>
```

✓ *Helps developers understand code faster*

Practice Lab Guide: Writing Clean HTML5 Code

Objective: Practice writing well-structured, semantic HTML5 code.

Steps to Follow:

1. Open a text editor (VS Code, Sublime Text, or Notepad++).
2. Create a new file and save it as clean-html.html.
3. Copy and paste this clean HTML code:

```
<!DOCTYPE html>
<html lang="en">
<head>
   <meta charset="UTF-8">
   <meta name="viewport" content="width=device-width, initial-scale=1.0">
   <title>Clean HTML Example</title>
</head>
<body>
```

```
<header>
  <h1>Welcome to My Clean HTML Page</h1>
</header>

<nav>
  <ul>
    <li><a href="#">Home</a></li>
    <li><a href="#">Services</a></li>
    <li><a href="#">Contact</a></li>
  </ul>
</nav>

<section>
  <h2>Our Services</h2>
  <p>We offer:</p>
  <ul>
    <li>Web Development</li>
    <li>SEO Optimization</li>
    <li>Graphic Design</li>
  </ul>
</section>
<footer>
  <p>&copy; 2025 My Website. All rights reserved.</p>
</footer>
</body>
</html>
```

4. Save and open the file in a web browser.
5. Modify the content to experiment with different tags and structures.

Conclusion

- HTML5 tags define and structure web content.
- Using semantic tags improves SEO, readability, and accessibility.
- Writing clean, well-organized HTML makes code easier to read and maintain.

Practice Lab Guide: Building a Simple Webpage with HTML5 Tags

Objective: Learn how to use HTML5 structural tags to create a simple, well-structured webpage.

Steps to Follow:

1. Open a text editor (e.g., Notepad++, VS Code, or Sublime Text).
2. Create a new file and save it as index.html.
3. Copy and paste the following code into your file:

```
<!DOCTYPE html>
<html lang="en">
<head>
  <meta charset="UTF-8">
  <meta name="viewport" content="width=device-width, initial-scale=1.0">
  <title>My HTML5 Page</title>
</head>
<body>
  <header>
    <h1>Welcome to My Site</h1>
  </header>
  <nav>
    <ul>
      <li><a href="#">Home</a></li>
```

```
        <li><a href="#">Services</a></li>
        <li><a href="#">Contact</a></li>
      </ul>
    </nav>
    <section>
      <h2>Our Services</h2>
      <p>We offer web development and design services.</p>
    </section>
    <aside>
      <p>Advertisement: Learn HTML5 Today!</p>
    </aside>
    <footer>
      <p>&copy; 2025 My Website. All rights reserved.</p>
    </footer>
  </body>
</html>
```

4. Save the file and open it in a web browser (Chrome, Firefox, Edge).
5. Experiment by changing text, adding more sections, or styling it with CSS.

Conclusion

HTML5 introduces new structural tags that improve readability, SEO, and accessibility. By using tags like <header>, <nav>, <section>, and <footer>, you can create well-organized and user-friendly webpages.

C. <u>New Elements in HTML5</u>

HTML5 introduced several new elements to improve webpage structure, readability, and functionality. These elements make web development more semantic, accessible, and efficient.

Structural Elements – Organizing Webpages

HTML5 provides better structure with new elements that clearly define different sections of a webpage.

Element	Purpose	Example
<header>	Represents the top section of a page or section (title, logo).	<header><h1>My Website</h1></header>
<nav>	Contains navigation links.	<nav><a href="#">Home</a></nav>
<section>	Groups related content.	<section><h2>About Us</h2></section>
<article>	Represents a self-contained piece of content (e.g. blog post).	<article><h2>News Update</h2></article>
<aside>	Holds related content like ads or links.	<aside>Related Articles</aside>
<footer>	Defines the bottom section of a page.	<footer>© 2025 My Website</footer>

Example: Basic Page Structure Using New Elements

```
<!DOCTYPE html>
<html lang="en">
<head>
  <meta charset="UTF-8">
  <meta name="viewport" content="width=device-width, initial-scale=1.0">
  <title>HTML5 Page Structure</title>
</head>
```

```
<body>
  <header>
    <h1>My Website</h1>
    <nav>
      <a href="#">Home</a> | <a href="#">Blog</a> | <a
href="#">Contact</a>
    </nav></header>

  <section>
    <h2>Welcome!</h2>
    <article>
      <h3>New Features in HTML5</h3>
      <p>HTML5 introduces many new tags that improve webpage
structure.</p>
    </article></section>

  <aside>
    <h3>Related Articles</h3>
    <ul>
      <li><a href="#">CSS3 Enhancements</a></li>
      <li><a href="#">JavaScript Updates</a></li>
    </ul>
  </aside>

  <footer>
    <p>&copy; 2025 My Website</p>
  </footer></body></html>
```

Advantage: Makes web pages more organized, readable, and SEO-friendly.

Multimedia Elements – Adding Audio & Video

HTML5 makes it easy to embed media files without third-party plugins (like Flash).

Element	Purpose	Example
`<audio>`	Embeds audio files.	`<audio controls src="music.mp3"></audio>`
`<video>`	Embeds video files.	`<video controls src="video.mp4"></video>`

Example: Adding Video & Audio

```
<audio controls>
    <source src="music.mp3" type="audio/mpeg">
    Your browser does not support the audio element.
</audio>
```

```
<video controls width="300">
    <source src="video.mp4" type="video/mp4">
    Your browser does not support the video tag.
</video>
```

Advantage: No need for Flash Player – works on all modern browsers.

Graphics Elements – Drawing with Code

HTML5 introduced `<canvas>` and `<svg>` to draw graphics, charts, and animations.

Element	Purpose	Example
`<canvas>`	Allows drawing using JavaScript.	`<canvas id="myCanvas"></canvas>`
`<svg>`	Creates scalable vector graphics.	`<svg><circle cx="50" cy="50" r="40" fill="blue"/></svg>`

Example: Drawing a Circle with <svg>

<svg width="100" height="100">

   <circle cx="50" cy="50" r="40" fill="blue"/>

</svg>

Advantage: Fast rendering and no image files needed!

Form Elements – Better User Input

HTML5 improves forms with new input types that make data entry easier.

Input Type	Purpose	Example
type="email"	Ensures email input is valid.	<input type="email">
type="date"	Provides a date picker.	<input type="date">
type="number"	Allows only numbers.	<input type="number" min="1" max="100">

Example: Simple HTML5 Form

<form>

   <label for="email">Email:</label>

   <input type="email" id="email" required>

   <label for="dob">Date of Birth:</label>

   <input type="date" id="dob">

   <button type="submit">Submit</button>

</form>

Advantage: Reduces errors and improves user experience.

Conclusion

- Why Are These Elements Important?
- Better structure for organizing content
- Improved multimedia support (audio/video)
- Enhanced graphics with <canvas> and <svg>
- Smarter forms with new input types

D. <u>HTML5 Event Attributes</u>

What is Event-Driven HTML?

HTML pages are typically static, but with event attributes, they can respond to user interactions.

What is an Event?

An event is an action triggered by the user (e.g., clicking a button) or the browser (e.g., page load).

Why Use Events?

- Enhances interactivity (e.g., button clicks, form submissions)
- Improves user experience (e.g., animations, dynamic content)
- Triggers JavaScript functions when users interact

Example: Basic Event Handling

<button onclick="alert('Button Clicked!')">Click Me</button>

When you click the button, an alert box appears saying "Button Clicked!"

Common Event Attributes

Event Attribute	Triggered When...	Example
onclick	User clicks an element	`<button onclick="alert('Hello!')">Click Me</button>`
onmouseover	Mouse moves over an element	`<p onmouseover="this.style.color='red'">Hover over me! </p>`
onmouseout	Mouse leaves an element	`<p onmouseout="this.style.color='black'">Hover to change color</p>`
onchange	Value of an input field changes	`<input type="text" onchange="alert('Value changed!')">`
onkeydown	A key is pressed down	`<input onkeydown="alert('Key Pressed!')">`
onload	Page or element finishes loading	`<body onload="alert('Page Loaded!')">`

Improving User Interaction with HTML Events

Event attributes make websites more interactive by responding to user actions.

Example 1: Changing Text Color on Hover (onmouseover & onmouseout)

```
<p onmouseover="this.style.color='blue'" onmouseout="this.style.color='black'">
    Hover over me to change my color!
</p>
```

- When you hover over the text, it turns blue.
- When you move the mouse away, it turns black again.

Example 2: Displaying an Alert on Input Change (onchange)

```
<input type="text" onchange="alert('You changed the text!')" placeholder="Type something...">
```

✔ *When you type something and press enter or click away, an alert appears.*

Example 3: Show/Hide a Message on Button Click (onclick)

```
<button
onclick="document.getElementById('message').style.display='block'">Show
Message</button>
<p id="message" style="display: none;">Hello! You clicked the button.</p>
```

✓ *When you click the button, a hidden message appears.*

Example 4: Dynamic Form Validation (onkeydown)

```
<input type="text" id="name" onkeydown="checkInput()" placeholder="Enter
your name">
<p id="warning" style="color: red; display: none;">Too short!</p>

<script>
   function checkInput() {
      let input = document.getElementById('name').value;
      if (input.length < 3) {
         document.getElementById('warning').style.display = 'block';
      } else {
         document.getElementById('warning').style.display = 'none';
      }
   }
</script>
```

✓ *If you type less than 3 characters, a warning message appears.*

Practice Lab Guide

- Create a new HTML file called event_attributes.html.
- Copy and paste the examples above.
- Modify the button event to display a custom message instead of an alert.
- Add an onmouseover event to change a paragraph's background color.
- Test the file in a browser to see how events make the page interactive.

Conclusion

- HTML5 event attributes make web pages interactive.
- They respond to user actions like clicks, typing, and hovering.
- Using JavaScript, events can trigger animations, validations, and more!

E. Integrating Google Maps with HTML5

Google Maps can be integrated into a webpage using HTML5 and JavaScript, allowing users to view locations, get directions, and interact with maps.

1. Embedding Maps in Web Pages

The simplest way to add a Google Map to a webpage is by using the Google Maps Embed API.

Steps to Embed a Map:

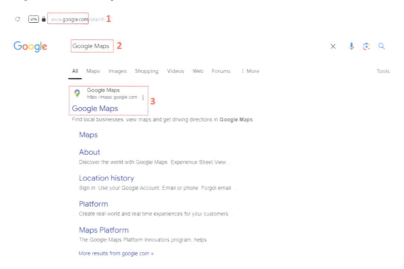

1. Open Google.com and search for Google Maps.
2. Search for a location (e.g., "New York").
3. Click Share → Embed a map.
4. Copy the <iframe> code.
5. Paste it into your HTML file.

Example: Embedding a Map

```
<!DOCTYPE html>
<html lang="en">
<head>
  <meta charset="UTF-8">
  <meta name="viewport" content="width=device-width, initial-scale=1.0">
  <title>Google Maps Embed</title>
</head>
<body>
  <h2>Our Location</h2>
  <iframe
     width="600"
     height="450"
     style="border:0;"
     loading="lazy"
     allowfullscreen
     referrerpolicy="no-referrer-when-downgrade"

src="https://www.google.com/maps/embed?pb=!1m18!1m12!1m3!1d3151.835434
5093703!2d144.95373631531793!3d-
37.816279442021664!2m3!1f0!2f0!3f0!3m2!1i1024!2i768!4f13.1!3m3!1m2!1s0x
6ad65d5df8f8f8f9%3A0x9a3b5764e15a662f!2sMelbourne%20VIC%2C%20Austr
alia!5e0!3m2!1sen!2sus!4v1644966267090!5m2!1sen!2sus">
  </iframe>
</body>
</html>
```

Advantage: *Quick and easy – no API key needed!*

2. Customizing Map Features

For more control, use the Google Maps JavaScript API to customize the map.

Features You Can Customize:

- Set the zoom level
- Define map types (roadmap, satellite, hybrid, terrain)
- Add markers to highlight locations

Example: Adding a Custom Map with a Marker

```html
<!DOCTYPE html>
<html lang="en">
<head>
  <meta charset="UTF-8">
  <meta name="viewport" content="width=device-width, initial-scale=1.0">
  <title>Google Maps Custom</title>
  <script
src="https://maps.googleapis.com/maps/api/js?key=YOUR_API_KEY&callback=
initMap" async defer></script>
  <script>
    function initMap() {
      var location = { lat: 37.7749, lng: -122.4194 }; // San Francisco
      var map = new google.maps.Map(document.getElementById("map"), {
        zoom: 12,
        center: location,
      });
      var marker = new google.maps.Marker({
        position: location,
        map: map,
        title: "San Francisco, CA"
```

```
        });
    }
  </script>
</head>
<body>
  <h2>Custom Google Map</h2>
  <div id="map" style="height: 400px; width: 100%;"></div>
</body>
</html>
```

Advantage: *More customization options and interactive features!*

3. Adding Interactive Location Services

Using the Geolocation API, you can get the user's location and display it on Google Maps.

How It Works:

1. The browser asks for location permission.
2. If allowed, it fetches the user's coordinates.
3. The location is displayed on the Google Map.

Example: Displaying the User's Location on Google Maps

```
<!DOCTYPE html>
<html lang="en">
<head>
  <meta charset="UTF-8">
  <meta name="viewport" content="width=device-width, initial-scale=1.0">
  <title>Google Maps with Geolocation</title>
```

```
<script
src="https://maps.googleapis.com/maps/api/js?key=YOUR_API_KEY&callback=
initMap" async defer></script>
<script>
  function initMap() {
    var map = new google.maps.Map(document.getElementById("map"), {
      zoom: 12,
      center: { lat: 0, lng: 0 }
    });

    if (navigator.geolocation) {
      navigator.geolocation.getCurrentPosition(function (position) {
        var userLocation = {
          lat: position.coords.latitude,
          lng: position.coords.longitude
        };
        map.setCenter(userLocation);
        new google.maps.Marker({
          position: userLocation,
          map: map,
          title: "You are here!"
        });
      });
    } else {
      alert("Geolocation is not supported by your browser.");
    }
  }
</script>
</head>
```

```
<body>
    <h2>Your Current Location</h2>
    <div id="map" style="height: 400px; width: 100%;"></div>
</body>
</html>
```

Advantage: Users can see their real-time location on the map!

Practice Lab Guide

1. Create an HTML file called google_maps_lab.html.
2. Copy & paste the basic embedded map example and view it in a browser.
3. Modify the iframe URL to show a different location.
4. Add a custom Google Map with a marker using the Google Maps JavaScript API.
5. Enable location tracking and test how it works.

Conclusion

- Embedding Google Maps is simple with an <iframe>.
- The JavaScript API allows full control over the map.
- Geolocation services make maps interactive and user-friendly.

F. HTML5 Semantics and Accessibility

HTML5 introduced semantic elements that improve SEO, readability, and accessibility for all users, including those using screen readers.

Why Semantic Elements Matter?

What Are Semantic Elements?

Semantic elements clearly describe their meaning in code, making it easier for developers and browsers to understand a webpage's structure.

Examples of Semantic vs. Non-Semantic Elements

Non-Semantic	Semantic	Why Use Semantic Elements?
<div>	<article>	Represents an independent article
<div>	<section>	Groups related content
<span>	<header>	Defines the page or section header
<div>	<footer>	Represents the page footer

- Better readability for developers
- Improved browser interpretation
- Easier maintenance

Example: Non-Semantic vs. Semantic Code

✗ Bad Example (Non-Semantic)

```
<div id="header">Welcome to My Website</div>
<div id="nav">
   <a href="#">Home</a>
   <a href="#">About</a>
</div>
```

```
<div id="content">This is an article.</div>
<div id="footer">Copyright 2025</div>
```

✓ Good Example (Semantic HTML)

```
<header>Welcome to My Website</header>
<nav>
    <a href="#">Home</a>
    <a href="#">About</a>
</nav>
<article>This is an article.</article>
<footer>Copyright 2025</footer>
```

✓ *Easier to read and better for accessibility!*

Improving SEO and User Experience

Semantic HTML helps search engines (Google, Bing) understand content structure, improving SEO rankings and user experience.

How Semantic HTML Helps SEO

- Search engines rank sites higher when content is well-structured
- Rich snippets appear in search results
- Faster page load time due to cleaner code

Example: Using <article> for SEO-Friendly Blog Posts

```
<article>
    <h2>Benefits of Semantic HTML</h2>
    <p>Semantic HTML improves SEO, accessibility, and readability...</p>
</article>
```

Creating Accessible Web Content

Accessibility ensures that websites can be used by people with disabilities, including those using screen readers.

Best Practices for Accessibility

- Use descriptive elements like <nav>, <main>, <aside>
- Include alt attributes for images
- Use ARIA attributes where needed

Example: Making Navigation Accessible

```
<nav aria-label="Main Navigation">
   <a href="#">Home</a>
   <a href="#">About</a>
</nav>
```

✅ Screen readers will read "Main Navigation" for visually impaired users!

Practice Lab Guide

1. Create an HTML file called semantic_accessibility.html
2. Use semantic tags (<header>, <article>, <footer>) instead of <div>
3. Test your page using an SEO tool like Google Lighthouse
4. Enable a screen reader (like NVDA or VoiceOver) and check accessibility

Conclusion

- Semantic HTML improves SEO, readability, and accessibility.
- Search engines and screen readers understand content better.
- Using the right elements creates a better web experience for everyone!

G. <u>Migrating to HTML5</u>

HTML5 is the latest version of HTML that introduces new elements, attributes, and APIs to improve web development. If you're moving from older versions like HTML4 or XHTML, you need to consider compatibility, performance, and best practices.

Transitioning from Older HTML Versions

When upgrading to HTML5, you need to replace outdated elements, adopt modern semantic tags, and remove unnecessary attributes.

Key Changes:

✅ **Doctype Simplification:** Replace <!DOCTYPE HTML PUBLIC "-//W3C//DTD HTML 4.01//EN"> with
<!DOCTYPE html>

✅ **Semantic Elements:** Use <header>, <article>, <section>, etc., instead of <div> for better readability.

✅ **Remove Deprecated Elements:** <font>, <center>, and <marquee> are no longer used.

✅ **New Form Features:** HTML5 adds new input types like email, date, and number.

Example - Before & After

✖ Old HTML4 Code:

```
<!DOCTYPE HTML PUBLIC "-//W3C//DTD HTML 4.01//EN">
<html>
  <head><title>My Page</title></head>
```

```
<body>
  <div align="center"><font color="red">Welcome</font></div>
</body>
</html>
```

✅ **Migrated to HTML5:**

```
<!DOCTYPE html>
<html>
  <head><title>My Page</title></head>
  <body>
    <header>
      <h1 style="color: red; text-align: center;">Welcome</h1>
    </header>
  </body>
</html>
```

Ensuring Compatibility with Legacy Browsers

Older browsers may not fully support HTML5, so you need fallbacks and polyfills.

Best Practices:

- Use Feature Detection with Modernizr: This helps check if a browser supports a feature before using it.
- Provide CSS Fallbacks: Use @supports or alternative styles for older browsers.
- Shiv for Older Browsers: Add this in <head> for IE8 and older:

```
<!--[if lt IE 9]>
```

```
<script
src="https://cdnjs.cloudflare.com/ajax/libs/html5shiv/3.7.3/html5shiv.min.js"></sc
ript>
<![endif]-->
```

Optimizing Code for Performance
HTML5 allows better page speed and efficiency with lightweight code.

Optimization Tips:
- Minimize HTTP Requests: Combine CSS and JavaScript files.
- Use <picture> for Responsive Images:

```
<picture>
  <source srcset="image-large.jpg" media="(min-width: 800px)">
  <source srcset="image-small.jpg" media="(max-width: 799px)">
  <img src="image-default.jpg" alt="Optimized Image">
</picture>
```

✅ Use Lazy Loading for Images:
```
<img src="image.jpg" loading="lazy" alt="Lazy Loaded Image">
```

✅ **Cache Static Content:** Use browser caching and Content Delivery Networks (CDNs).

Practice Lab Guide

Lab 1: Upgrade an Old HTML4 Page to HTML5

Steps:

1. Open an old HTML4 file.
2. Change the doctype to <!DOCTYPE html>.
3. Replace <div> structures with semantic HTML5 tags.
4. Remove deprecated elements.
5. Test on multiple browsers.

Lab 2: Check Browser Compatibility

Steps:

1. Open a modern HTML5 page in an older browser (IE8 or below).
2. Use Modernizr to detect missing features.
3. Add necessary polyfills and fallback CSS.

Lab 3: Optimize for Performance

Steps:

1. Use a large image and apply lazy loading.
2. Minify HTML, CSS, and JavaScript using an online tool like Minifier.
3. Check page speed with Google PageSpeed Insights and optimize accordingly.

By following these steps, you can successfully migrate to HTML5 while ensuring compatibility and improving performance!

H. Using Audio in HTML5

Adding Sound with the <audio> Element

The <audio> tag is used to add sound effects, background music, or voice recordings to a webpage. It supports multiple audio formats and provides playback controls.

Basic Syntax:

```
<audio controls>
    <source src="audio.mp3" type="audio/mpeg">
    <source src="audio.ogg" type="audio/ogg">
    Your browser does not support the audio element.
</audio>
```

Explanation:

- controls: Displays play, pause, and volume options.
- source: Specifies different audio formats to ensure cross-browser support.
- Fallback Text: If the browser doesn't support <audio>, it shows a message.

Supported Audio Formats

Different browsers support different audio file formats, so it's best to include multiple formats.

Format	File Extension	Browser Support
MP3	.mp3	Chrome, Firefox, Safari, Edge, Opera
Ogg Vorbis	.ogg	Chrome, Firefox, Opera
WAV	.wav	Chrome, Firefox, Safari, Edge

Customizing Audio Controls and Playback

HTML5 allows developers to customize the audio player using attributes, JavaScript, and CSS.

Attributes for <audio>

- autoplay: Starts playing automatically.
- loop: Repeats the audio after it ends.
- muted: Starts the audio in a muted state.
- preload: Controls how the audio loads (auto, metadata, none).

Example with Attributes:

```
<audio controls autoplay loop>
    <source src="background.mp3" type="audio/mpeg">
</audio>
```

Customizing with JavaScript

JavaScript can control playback, volume, and other interactions.

```
<audio id="myAudio">
    <source src="sound.mp3" type="audio/mpeg">
</audio>
<button onclick="playAudio()">Play</button>
<button onclick="pauseAudio()">Pause</button>
<script>
    var audio = document.getElementById("myAudio");
    function playAudio() {
        audio.play();
    }
    function pauseAudio() {
```

```
        audio.pause();
    }
</script>
```

Styling with CSS: The default <audio> player can be hidden and replaced with a custom UI.

```
audio { width: 300px;
    border-radius: 10px;
}
```

Practice Lab Guide

Lab 1: Embed an Audio File

Objective: Add a playable audio file to a webpage.

Steps:

1. Create an HTML file.
2. Use the <audio> tag to embed an MP3 file.
3. Add controls to enable play/pause.
4. Test in different browsers.

Lab 2: Create a Custom Audio Player

Objective: Control audio playback using JavaScript.

Steps:

1. Add an <audio> element with an MP3 file.
2. Create custom play and pause buttons.
3. Use JavaScript to control playback.

By using these techniques, you can easily add and customize audio on your web pages!

Miquill Nyle

I. <u>Working with Video in HTML5</u>

HTML5 introduced the <video> element, allowing developers to embed and control videos without relying on third-party plugins like Flash. This makes it easier to include videos that work across different devices and browsers.

Embedding Video Using the <video> Element
The <video> tag is used to add videos to a webpage. It supports multiple formats and provides built-in controls.

Basic Syntax:

```
<video controls width="600">
   <source src="video.mp4" type="video/mp4">
   <source src="video.ogg" type="video/ogg">
   Your browser does not support the video tag.
</video>
```

Explanation:
- controls: Displays play, pause, volume, and fullscreen options.
- width="600": Sets the width of the video.
- source: Multiple formats ensure compatibility with different browsers.
- Fallback Text: If the browser doesn't support <video>, it shows a message.

Other Useful Attributes:
- autoplay: Starts playing automatically.
- loop: Repeats the video after it ends.
- muted: Starts the video in a muted state.
- poster: Displays an image before the video plays.

Example with attributes:

<video controls autoplay loop muted poster="thumbnail.jpg" width="600">

   <source src="video.mp4" type="video/mp4">

</video>

Supported Video Formats and Codecs

Different browsers support different video formats, so it's best to include multiple formats.

Format	File Extension	Browser Support
MP4 (H.264)	.mp4	Chrome, Firefox, Safari, Edge, Opera
WebM (VP8/VP9)	.webm	Chrome, Firefox, Edge, Opera
Ogg Theora	.ogv	Firefox, Opera

Best Practice: Use MP4 (H.264) for maximum compatibility.

Adding Subtitles and Captions for Accessibility

Subtitles (for different languages) and captions (for the hearing impaired) improve accessibility.

Adding Subtitles with the <track> Element

<video controls width="600">

   <source src="video.mp4" type="video/mp4">

   <track src="subtitles-en.vtt" kind="subtitles" srclang="en" label="English">

   <track src="subtitles-es.vtt" kind="subtitles" srclang="es" label="Spanish">

</video>

Explanation:

- <track>: Adds subtitles or captions.
- src="subtitles-en.vtt": Links to a WebVTT subtitle file.

- kind="subtitles": Specifies that these are subtitles.
- srclang="en": Defines the language of the subtitles.
- label="English": Names the subtitle option in the player.

Example WebVTT (.vtt) File (subtitles-en.vtt)

WEBVTT

00:00:00.000 --> 00:00:05.000

Welcome to our video tutorial.

00:00:05.001 --> 00:00:10.000

In this lesson, we'll learn about HTML5 videos.

Practice Lab Guide

Lab 1: Embed a Video

Objective: Add a playable video to a webpage.

Steps:

1. Create an HTML file.
2. Use the <video> tag to embed an MP4 file.
3. Add controls to enable play/pause.
4. Test in different browsers.

Lab 2: Add Subtitles to a Video

Objective: Improve accessibility with captions.

Steps:

1. Create a WebVTT file (subtitles.vtt).
2. Link it to a <video> element using <track>.
3. Test subtitles in different browsers.

J. Scalable Vector Graphics (SVG) in HTML5

SVG (Scalable Vector Graphics) is an XML-based format for creating images that can be scaled without losing quality. Unlike raster images (JPEG, PNG), SVG graphics remain sharp at any size.

Working with Video in HTML5Introduction to SVG

SVG is a markup language used to define vector graphics directly within an

HTML document. It is useful for logos, icons, charts, and interactive graphics.

Basic Syntax:

```
<svg width="200" height="200">
   <circle cx="100" cy="100" r="50" stroke="black" stroke-width="3" fill="red"
/>
</svg>
```

Explanation:

- <svg>: Defines the SVG container.
- <circle>: Draws a circle with:
- cx="100": X position of center
- cy="100": Y position of center
- r="50": Radius
- stroke="black": Border color
- stroke-width="3": Border thickness
- fill="red": Inside color

Creating and Editing SVG Graphics

SVG images can be created manually using code or designed using tools like

Adobe Illustrator, Inkscape, or online SVG editors.

Example: Drawing a Rectangle

```
<svg width="300" height="200">
    <rect x="50" y="50" width="200" height="100" fill="blue" stroke="black"
stroke-width="3"/>
</svg>
```

Explanation:

- <rect>: Draws a rectangle
- x="50", y="50": Position
- width="200", height="100": Size
- fill="blue": Background color
- stroke="black", stroke-width="3": Border

Editing SVG in Code vs. Software:

- In Code: You can modify SVG elements in an HTML file.
- In Software: Create a design in Illustrator or Inkscape and export as .svg.

Benefits of SVG Over Traditional Image Formats

Feature	SVG	PNG/JPG
Scalability	Infinite scaling without quality loss	Becomes pixelated when enlarged
File Size	Smaller for simple graphics	Larger due to pixel data
Interactivity	Can be animated and styled with CSS/JS	Static images only
Performance	Faster rendering for vector graphics	Heavy on performance for large images
Editability	Can be modified in text editors	Requires Photoshop or Illustrator

Practice Lab Guide

Lab 1: Create Basic SVG Shapes

Objective: Draw shapes using SVG in HTML.

Steps:

1. Open an HTML file.
2. Add <svg> with a <circle> and <rect>.
3. Customize colors and sizes.
4. Open in a browser to see results.

Lab 2: Edit an SVG File

Objective: Modify an SVG created in a graphics tool.

Steps:

1. Create an SVG file in Inkscape or Illustrator.
2. Open the .svg file in a text editor.
3. Modify the color or shape size in the code.
4. Reload the file to see changes.

By learning SVG, you can create high-quality, scalable graphics for websites with interactive effects!

K. HTML5 Canvas for Graphics and Animations

The **<canvas>** element in HTML5 allows developers to create dynamic graphics, animations, and interactive content using JavaScript. It is widely used for game development, data visualization, and interactive web applications.

Understanding the <canvas> Element

The <canvas> element provides a drawing area where you can render 2D graphics using JavaScript.

Basic Syntax:

<canvas id="myCanvas" width="400" height="200" style="border:1px solid black;"></canvas>

Explanation:

- <canvas>: Defines a drawing space.
- id="myCanvas": Unique identifier to access it via JavaScript.
- width="400" height="200": Specifies dimensions.
- style="border:1px solid black;": Adds a visible border (optional).

Canvas alone does nothing! JavaScript is required to draw graphics.

Drawing Shapes and Lines with JavaScript

To draw on the canvas, we need to use JavaScript and access its context.

Basic Steps:

1. Get the canvas element using JavaScript.
2. Get the 2D rendering context (getContext("2d")).

3. Use drawing functions to create shapes.

Example: Drawing a Line

```
<canvas id="myCanvas" width="400" height="200"></canvas>
<script>
  var canvas = document.getElementById("myCanvas");
  var ctx = canvas.getContext("2d");

  ctx.moveTo(50, 50); // Start position
  ctx.lineTo(200, 150); // End position
  ctx.stroke(); // Draw the line
</script>
```

Example: Drawing a Rectangle

```
<canvas id="myCanvas" width="400" height="200"></canvas>
<script>
  var canvas = document.getElementById("myCanvas");
  var ctx = canvas.getContext("2d");

  ctx.fillStyle = "blue"; // Set color
  ctx.fillRect(50, 50, 150, 100); // (x, y, width, height)
</script>
```

Developing Interactive and Animated Graphics

Canvas can create animations by repeatedly drawing frames using requestAnimationFrame().

Example: Moving a Ball Animation

```
<canvas id="myCanvas" width="400" height="200"></canvas>
```

```
<script>
    var canvas = document.getElementById("myCanvas");
    var ctx = canvas.getContext("2d");

    var x = 50;  // Starting position
    var y = 100;
    var dx = 2;  // Speed

    function drawBall() {
        ctx.clearRect(0, 0, canvas.width, canvas.height); // Clear previous frame
        ctx.beginPath();
        ctx.arc(x, y, 20, 0, Math.PI * 2); // Draw ball
        ctx.fillStyle = "red";
        ctx.fill();
        ctx.closePath();

        x += dx; // Move ball
        if (x > canvas.width - 20 || x < 20) dx = -dx; // Reverse direction if it hits the edge
        requestAnimationFrame(drawBall); // Call function again for next frame
    }
    drawBall(); // Start animation
</script>
```

Explanation:
- clearRect(): Clears the previous frame before drawing a new one.
- arc(): Draws a ball (circle).
- requestAnimationFrame(drawBall): Calls drawBall() repeatedly to create animation.

- Direction Change: The ball bounces when it reaches the canvas edge.

Practice Lab Guide

Lab 1: Draw Shapes with Canvas
Objective: Create basic shapes (line, rectangle, circle).
Steps:
1. Create an HTML file with a <canvas> element.
2. Write JavaScript to draw different shapes.
3. Experiment with colors and sizes.

Lab 2: Create an Interactive Drawing Board
Objective: Allow users to draw with the mouse.
Steps:
1. Detect mouse movements using JavaScript.
2. Draw lines on the canvas where the mouse moves.
3. Add color selection and clear button.

Lab 3: Make an Animated Object
Objective: Move a shape across the canvas.
Steps:
1. Draw a shape (like a ball).
2. Update its position in a loop.
3. Use requestAnimationFrame() to animate it.

By learning the <canvas> element, you can create interactive web graphics and animations for games, visual effects, and dynamic content!

L. Final Laboratory Test: HTML5 Comprehensive Exam

Objective:
This final lab test assesses your ability to apply various HTML5 concepts, including structuring web content, implementing multimedia elements, using semantic tags, handling events, and integrating interactive elements such as Google Maps, SVG, and Canvas graphics.

Instructions:
1. **Create an HTML file (final_lab.html)** that demonstrates all the required topics.
2. **Use proper HTML5 structure** and best practices.
3. **Enhance interactivity** with JavaScript where required.
4. **Style your page** with CSS for readability and aesthetics.
5. **Test your code** in multiple browsers to ensure compatibility.

Tasks and Requirements
1. HTML5 Tags and Structure
- Create a valid HTML5 document.
- Use <article>, <section>, <header>, <footer>, <nav>, and <aside> appropriately.
- Maintain clean and well-indented code.

2. New Elements in HTML5
- Inside the <body>, include:
  - A <header> with a site title.
  - A <nav> with links to different sections.
  - An <article> containing sample blog content.
  - A <footer> with copyright information.

3. HTML5 Event Attributes
- Add buttons and interactive elements that use event attributes:
  - A button with an onclick event to display an alert.
  - An input field with an onchange event to display typed text.
  - A <div> that changes color when hovered using onmouseover.

4. Integrating Google Maps
- Embed a Google Map showing a specific location.
- Customize the map (e.g., zoom level, markers).
- Include a button to switch to satellite view.

5. HTML5 Semantics and Accessibility
- Use semantic tags correctly for better SEO and accessibility.
- Include proper alt attributes for images.
- Ensure the webpage is navigable via keyboard.

6. Migrating to HTML5
- Show an example of old <div>-based structure transitioning to semantic elements.
- Include a fallback message for older browsers that do not support HTML5 features.
- Optimize loading performance using best practices.

7. Using Audio in HTML5
- Embed an audio player using the <audio> element.
- Provide at least two supported formats (MP3, OGG).
- Include controls such as play, pause, and volume.

8. Working with Video in HTML5
- Embed a video using the <video> tag.
- Include multiple formats (MP4, WebM).
- Add subtitles using the <track> element.

9. Scalable Vector Graphics (SVG) in HTML5
- Include an inline SVG drawing (e.g., a circle or rectangle).
- Modify the SVG element's size and color using CSS.
- Show the benefits of SVG over PNG/JPG.

10. HTML5 Canvas for Graphics and Animations
- Create a <canvas> element.
- Draw at least two shapes using JavaScript.
- Implement a simple animation (e.g., a moving ball).

Congratulations!

You've successfully completed the journey through HTML5 and mastered its many powerful features. Your dedication to learning and your commitment to honestly performing each task have truly paid off.

By exploring semantic elements, integrating multimedia, enhancing interactivity, and creating dynamic graphics, you've built a solid foundation in modern web development. Keep pushing forward, continue to innovate, and remember that each line of code you write contributes to a better, more accessible web for everyone.

Well done, and here's to many more achievements in your coding journey!

Miquill Nyle

Book Synopsis

In an era where web development is constantly evolving, **Mastering HTML5** serves as an essential guide for both beginners and experienced developers who want to harness the full potential of HTML5. This book provides a structured and in-depth exploration of modern HTML5 features, best practices, and powerful integrations that shape today's web experiences.

Through clear explanations, real-world examples, and interactive exercises, this book covers **HTML5 structure, semantics, multimedia, graphics, interactivity, and accessibility**—helping readers build cleaner, more efficient, and more engaging web applications.

~Miquill Nyle

www.ingramcontent.com/pod-product-compliance
Lightning Source LLC
LaVergne TN
LVHW072051060326
832903LV00054B/402